Original title:
Beneath the Grow Light

Copyright © 2025 Creative Arts Management OÜ
All rights reserved.

Author: Penelope Hawthorne
ISBN HARDBACK: 978-1-80581-868-7
ISBN PAPERBACK: 978-1-80581-395-8
ISBN EBOOK: 978-1-80581-868-7

Flourishing in a Tender Glow

In a room where veggies giggle,
Their leaves all dance and wiggle,
Tomatoes blush with a cheeky grin,
Dreaming of the salad win.

Radishes laugh, they're quite the jest,
Saying, 'We're the crunchiest, the best!'
With herbs that twirl in leafy caps,
Chasing away their sleepy naps.

The Light that Nurtures

Oh, the glow that's bright and bold,
Makes even cacti feel quite sold,
Lettuce leans back, gets a good tan,
Declaring, 'Look, I'm the shining plan!'

Peppers blush, thinking they're stars,
While sprouts discuss their future cars,
Every seed's got a comedy act,
In this greenhouse, laughter's packed!

Heartbeats under Glass

Inside the dome of glass and cheer,
Plants are plotting, never fear,
Beans are drumming, beats so sweet,
While little shoots tap their tiny feet.

Zucchinis dream of the gala night,
Wearing dresses of pure delight,
Spinach prances with leafy flair,
Whispering secrets to the air.

Vibrant Isolation

In their private leafy club,
Chill lettuce gives a friendly rub,
Talking radishes, oh what sass,
Each gossiping through shimmering glass.

Carrots wiggle, saying 'We're cool!'
While basil thinks it runs the school,
In this vibrant world of green,
Every leaf knows what fun should mean!

Radiant Harvests

In a garden where socks are the norm,
Tomatoes giggle, growing in swarm.
They bask in the glow, do cartwheels of cheer,
As lettuce whispers, "Let's all persevere!"

The cucumbers dance with a comical flair,
Wearing shades and enjoying fresh air.
They joke about salads, the leafy brigade,
While peas pull pranks, unafraid of the shade.

Under the Dome of Light

In a dome that's bright, like a neon sign,
Carrots tell stories, sipping on wine.
With radishes laughing, knocking on wood,
They cheer for each sprout, as best as they could.

The herbs play cards, all packed in a row,
While the chives exchange gossip, a real garden show.
Under this brilliance, they plot and they scheme,
A party of plants, living the dream.

Dreams in Hydroponic Gardens

In a tank filled with giggles and splashes of green,
Lettuce dons goggles, a sight to be seen.
"Dive in!" shouts the basil, flipping with glee,
While watercress swims, shouting, "Look at me!"

They float and they frolic, creating a scene,
With aquaponic fish as the finest cuisine.
In dreams of their harvest, they barter and wheel,
All for a salad, the underwater meal!

Tending to the Luminal

In the glow of their haven, the veggies unite,
As zucchini jokes spark with pure delight.
"Why did the tomato blush?" they all laugh aloud,
"Because it saw the salad dressing, so proud!"

The peppers share puns, a zesty brigade,
While carrots reenact the dance of parade.
In their luminal world with this jolly crew,
Each day's a festival, a comedy too!

The Pulse of Photosynthesis

In a room where the plants do dance,
They wiggle and wiggle, not missing a chance.
Photos fuel their delight, oh what a sight,
They work on their tans, from morning till night.

With lights like the sun, they're feeling so bold,
In their leafy parade, a sight to behold.
The smiles they wear, quite absurd, it's true,
A chlorophyll party, just for a few!

Cradled in Arcane Light

Oh, the glow from above makes them sway and humm,
A leafy ruckus, just taste the fun!
With petals like dancers, they jive and they spin,
In this leafy cabaret, it's a real win-win!

They drink from their cups filled with glimmers and beams,
Living the life of their plant-based dreams.
A photosynthetic rave, no need to invite,
They are the stars here, thriving in light.

Whispers of the Photosynthetic Night

As night falls and moonlight starts to play,
The plants cast their shadows in a funny ballet.
They whisper sweet secrets with leaves all aglow,
Chlorophyll laughter, oh how they bestow!

The ferns have their gossip, while cacti just grin,
They tell tales of sunshine where the fun begins.
In the hush of the moon, they giggle and cheer,
Plant dreams take flight, with no sadness near.

Shadows of Verdant Dreams

In the shadows, the greens bloom with glee,
Dancing in rhythms, just plants being free.
The lettuce does limbo, the thyme does a twist,
In this verdant disco, no one can resist!

A sprout with a swagger, a petal with sass,
In this leafy riot, they're all first class.
They laugh at the moon; they giggle at stars,
In the garden of dreams, there're no such bars!

In Shades of Bright Green

In a jungle of pots, they preen,
Lettuce and herbs in a merry routine.
Chasing the beams like sun-crazed cats,
Who knew plants liked jokes? Oh, what of that!

With chlorophyll dreams in each leafy head,
They giggle and wiggle, but stay in their bed.
Tomatoes roll dice, with basil as judge,
While kale cracks a joke and gives a small shrug.

Symphony of Growth Under Glass

A chorus of greens in bright harmony,
Strumming the light like a grand symphony.
The violets dance while the mint sings out,
In this leafy farce, there's no shadow of doubt.

Each sprout has a tale, oh so witty and wild,
Spinach cracks jokes, and zucchini just smiled.
In pots they conspire, a showbiz delight,
Who knew plants had dreams every day and night?

The Unseen Sun Above

The sun has a riddle; oh, what is its game?
Causing seedlings to stretch, yet none feel the shame.
They squint and they stretch, a comical sight,
Chasing the shadows that dance with delight.

Giggling leaves hum tunes about light and shade,
With mischief and charm, they all serenade.
Basil claims victory, a true sunlight champ,
While cacti just sit, feeling quite like a lamp.

Light's Gentle Caress Amidst Plant Life

A soft beam of warmth, like a blanket of glee,
Wraps all the green sprouts, as snug as can be.
They wiggle and giggle, with radiance grand,
In this lively city of leaf and of hand.

Moss dances gently, a waltz with the sun,
While carrots play pranks, having so much fun.
Each bloom shares its laughter, its color, its cheer,
In this planty parade, it's the best time of year!

Envisioning Verdancy

In a room where plants conspire,
Green dreams dance on wires.
Silly leaves in sunshine swoon,
Like disco balls, they groon.

A cactus wearing glasses, so chic,
Sips on water, just a week.
Pansies gossip, petals a-flutter,
While succulents giggle at lunchtime clutter.

Another sprout with a wild hairdo,
Claims it's the latest fashion, too.
Their soil is full of laughter's grit,
In this party, they're fully lit.

When light beams down in playful streaks,
Nature's nursery has all the freaks.
With every inch they stretch and dance,
A comedy show in green expanse.

The Glow-Woven Stories

Once a fern spun tales of old,
With every frond, bright and bold.
Whispers float in the warm embrace,
As each petal beams with a smiley face.

A tomato blushes, shrugs with glee,
Saying, "I'm ripe, come dine with me!"
Meanwhile, ivy boasts of its climb,
"I'm the real deal, a green paradigm!"

Lights flicker, the breeze goes 'whoosh!'
Sprouts bounce around, a leafy rush.
In this garden, jokes bloom wide,
As laughter sprinkles like morning tide.

So gather 'round, let stories unfold,
In the glow, where cheer takes hold.
Each leaf a sage, each root a plot,
Nature's sitcom, a lively lot.

Nature's Tapestry of Light

In a patch where sunshine plays,
Plants wear outfits, bright arrays.
Bamboo poses with style and flair,
While cacti practice their cool, just rare.

A sunflower stands tall, oh so proud,
Mimicking poses of a merry crowd.
Geranium winks, with petals aglow,
Saying, "Dance with me, let's steal the show!"

When night creeps in, they whisper sly,
"Did you see how that bean sprout did fly?"
With laughter woven through vines so sweet,
Nature's laughter erupts on repeat.

So sail with blooms, let your spirit soar,
Join the fiesta, there's fun galore!
In this bright stage, every moment shines,
In the glow of love, our joy entwines.

Perceptions of the Botanical Soul

In the calm of the light's embrace,
A plant does a funny little race.
With roots that tickle, it leaps about,
Making friends with a worm named Scout.

Rhythmic soil taps like a beat,
Each sprout's rhythm, oh so sweet.
Fungi giggle from mossy spots,
As they share jokes in sudsy pots.

A plastic fern claims it's the queen,
Sipping on sunshine, what a scene!
While daisies roll with laughter so bright,
In a world where plant dreams take flight.

So let your green thumb grow to play,
In the garden where whimsy stays.
In every petal, a universe spins,
With humor as vibrant as the blooms within.

Photosynthetic Whispers

In a room where plants giggle,
Photosynthesis dances, oh so simple.
Leaves chat in green, with a wink and a glow,
Sipping sunlight, putting on quite a show.

A cactus told secrets, round and round,
While ferns shared their gossip in whispers profound.
A daisy declared, with petals so bright,
"I bloom for the laughs, not just for the light!"

Luminescent Eden

Under the glow of electric skies,
Plants play charades—what a funny surprise!
A sprout in the corner, wearing sunglasses bold,
Exclaims, "I'm thriving, if truth be told!"

With bulbs that chuckle and fixtures that cheer,
Photosynthesis parties, bringing good cheer.
Lettuce in laughter, a broccoli shimmies,
Together they sway like animated skimmies.

Nurtured in Warmth

Warmth wraps the leaves, in cozy embrace,
As plants share jokes in a leafy space.
An orchid shyly whispers a pun,
"Why did the tomato turn red? Just for fun!"

A leafy lark with a flair for delight,
Tells tales of the sun that peeked in at night.
Each sprout and each bloom, full of quirk and glee,
Finds joy in the warmth, just wait and see!

Secrets Among the Leaves

In a jungle of colors, secrets unfold,
Where leaves tell stories, they never get old.
"I'm a fan of the light," said the sweet pea with pride,
"But I'll never forget where my laughs still reside!"

A sinister vine with a dramatic flair,
Said, "Grow up, folks, it's a comedy air!"
Peeking from shadows, with roots underground,
Here blooms a garden where humor is found.

Chlorophyll and Lightwaves

Chlorophyll's a party, oh what fun,
Lightwaves dance in, making everyone run.
Photosynthesis, come and take a chance,
Turn those rays into a leafy dance!

Grow lights flicker, like a disco ball,
Plants shimmy and sway, having a ball.
Green little dancers, they're quite the sight,
In this leafy rave, all feels just right.

Flora's Tender Awakening

Waking up slowly, the plants feel bright,
Sipping some sunlight, what a delight!
With petals all perky, and stems so gay,
They laugh at the clouds, 'Don't rain on our day!'

Chirping crickets, they join in the cheer,
As sprouts crack a joke, 'We're so glad you're here!'
Dewdrops like glitter on leaves full of grace,
Flora in Bloom, that's the ultimate place!

Night's Embrace Under Brightness

In a world where shadows are merely a prank,
The plants hold a party, in rows on the bank.
'Is it night?' one asks, with a twinkling leaf,
'Nah, we're just vibing, beyond all belief!'

With moonbeams giggling, they sway to their beat,
Cacti tell tales about growing their feet.
They've traded the dark for a glow that's so bright,
In the garden of grins, everything feels right!

The Geometric Growth of Green

Triangles and circles, what a strange sight,
Plants plot their growth under beams of pure light.
Calculating angles, they stretch and they bend,
'Is this math class? Or are we just friends?'

A square-root of laughter, exponential joy,
Leafy equations that nobody can destroy.
In this geometry, they're kings and they're queens,
All sprouting together, the ruler of greens!

Radiance of the Unseen

In a world where veggies dance,
They twirl and sway, it's quite a prance.
Tomatoes laugh, cucumbers tease,
Growing tall with such great ease.

The peppers flash their vibrant hues,
While hidden roots have secret dues.
Radishes play peek-a-boo games,
Each one with its own silly names.

Laughing leaves begin to sing,
As sunlight beams and shadows cling.
Carrots whisper from their beds,
Sharing dreams inside their heads.

A leafy parade, what a sight,
Underneath the faux daylight.
With every seedling's eager shout,
Who knew growing could be this sprout!

Flora's Gentle Embrace

In pots where laughter's freely grown,
Plants gossip tales in hushed tone.
'Why do we bloom?' one asked a bud,
'Is it for beauty or just for fun mud?'

Herbs chat about the spice of life,
Debating garlic's hubris and strife.
The parsley shakes with froggy cheer,
While basil jokes, 'Who's the fairest here?'

Succulents lounge with serene grace,
Taking selfies, oh what a place!
Sipping sunlight, sipping dreams,
Exploring how low a cactus seems.

A treasure trove of leafy wit,
In every pot, a giggle fit.
With roots entangled, wild and bright,
Who knew plants could share such delight?

Essence of the Light-Drenched Soil

In the soil where giggles grow,
Wiggly worms put on a show.
They twist and turn with flair and glee,
Mud must be quite the joyful spree!

Seeds tell stories in the dark,
Planning trips to the sunflower park.
They dream of sun, of rain, of fun,
While dirt-clad socks run on the run.

Daisies debate, 'Should I be white?'
'Or add some pink, for extra bite?'
The daisies sport their vibrant coats,
Cheering for their planty votes.

In heavy pots where all reside,
A riotous bloom, no need to hide.
For roots that laugh and leaves so bright,
It's a plant party, oh what a sight!

The Cultivation of Shadowed Glow

In moonlight's glow, the plants conspire,
Whispering secrets, their hearts afire.
'What if we danced under the stars?'
A daring plan for all of ours.

Night blooms twinkle with silly mirth,
Claiming their spots in the vast earth.
'What's that over there?' one fearfully said,
'A gnome? Or a broccoli with a head?'

The ferns sway wildly, a couple excels,
Breathing in stories, casting the spells.
With shadows stretching, the laughter flies,
Under the moonlit canvas of skies.

A garden fest from dusk till dawn,
Where roots and shoots are best of pals drawn.
In the cultivation of playful light,
All join in, and it feels so right!

Tendrils of Transcendence

In a jungle of plastic, we do sprout,
Give us a dose of laughter, no doubt!
Dancing in sunlight, a green little crew,
Spinning tales like we're growing anew.

With roots that are tangled and giggles that shout,
We bicker like veggies, what's that about?
Photosynthesizing dreams, oh what a sight,
Growing puns and laughter, day turns to night.

The Warmth of Cultivation

Oh, the warmth of the glow so sweet and bright,
Chasing shadows and critters, what a flight!
Watering cans chuckle, soil's having a ball,
Whispering to daisies, don't trip, don't fall!

Spritz on the mist, we shimmy and dance,
In a chlorophyll party, all plants take a chance.
With cacti in hats and ferns in a line,
Even the weeds think they're looking divine!

Sprouting Under Enchanted Rays

Under beams of magic, the schrooms sway,
Singing with joy, not a grumpy bouquet!
Tomatoes in shades, they joke 'about ripe,'
While lettuce chats gossip on crispy green hype.

With radishes whistling a jolly old tune,
And carrots in tutus, they'll dance to the moon.
Herbs baking jokes in the warm, soft glow,
Life's quite a feast as we all put on a show!

Life's Subtle Struggles

A sprout in the pot, oh what a tight squeeze,
Trying to stretch with the greatest of ease.
But how can one grow when the soil's a mess?
We laugh through the struggle, who needs all that stress?

With bending and twisting, we learn to adapt,
In this wild little dance, there's naught to be trapped.
Chasing after sunlight, giggles in the breeze,
Plant pals united, we grow as we please!

Luminescent Roots

In a pot of black soil, they dance and sway,
Roots doing a jig, come join in the play!
With a sip of some water, and instant cheer,
Yeah, take that, you weeds—I'm the star here!

They wiggle and wriggle, too happy to stay,
Planting their feet in a very odd way.
"Look at me glow!" one vine starts to tease,
You can't catch my moves, I'll grow like a breeze!

When the sun gets tired and the night comes around,
They tell tales of light in a giggly sound.
"My leaves are a party, come see me all night,
I'm the disco of gardens, feeling so right!"

So if you should wander where the plants misbehave,
You'll find laughter and roots that just can't be shaved.
With a twist and a turn, they'll grow with a jest,
In the garden of fun, they are simply the best!

The Glow in Greenhouses

In the greenhouse corner, strange shadows do lie,
Cucumbers chuckle, while carrots just sigh.
Tomatoes in linen, they think they're so grand,
Acting like royalty, just like they planned.

"Hey, Lettuce," says Radish, "Do you feel that vibe?"
The fluorescent fixture is alive with the tribe.
Beans boast about climbing, while peas just sleep in,
But the zinnias giggle, dressed in a spin!

Cacti complain, "Hey, what's with your glow?
We're pokey and prickly, but still can't steal show!"
Each plant has its charm, a hilarious sight,
In the greenhouse dance, they shine oh so bright.

So grab a chair, sit with all of your friends,
The laughter grows louder, the fun never ends.
In this odd little world where plants can unite,
Let's toast to green thumbs and their glowing delight!

Emerald Hues After Dusk

As the sun sinks low and the shadows grow wide,
Cabbages plot all the ways they can hide.
"Quick! Cover my leaves!" squeaks a young sprout,
While kale starts to giggle, "Come on, scream and shout!"

Under cover of twilight, they twirl and they prance,
Strawberries sing songs, giving night a chance.
"Did you hear that?" whispers the sage to the thyme,
"It's the sound of my thoughts, let's dance on a dime!"

The moon's a big lightbulb on a mischievous spree,
Shining down on mishaps of plants wild and free.
"Chill out, my friends!" says the wise old oak,
"Let's have a jam session, just trust me, no joke!"

So when night falls softly, and all seems quite right,
Join the plants in their carols—what a joyous sight!
With emerald hues twinkling under lunar hue,
These greens in the night share their laughter with you.

Chlorophyll's Serenade

Oh, chlorophyll, darling, your dance is so spry,
Swinging in sunlight, like you're gonna fly!
"Watch out!" warns the celery, "We might take a leap,
Sway to the rhythm; no time for sleep!"

The garden's a stage, with daisies in rows,
Marigolds cheer, where everyone grows.
"Let's hold a concert," croons the bright little beet,
While radish strums music with roots, oh so sweet!

"Did you ever see carrots get funky and twist?"
They hop and they jiggle, oh, you get the gist!
With petals all flashing and vines on parade,
This is how green friends do their serenade.

So next time you wander by gardens so lush,
Listen closely for whispers in that leafy hush.
For under the sun, in their jolly brigade,
The plants are all singing, come join the charade!

Illuminations in Soil and Sky

In a room where plants discuss,
They boast of sun, but it's just us.
With fluorescent gleam, they twist and sway,
Convinced it's summer every day.

The ferns sneak glances, the cacti wink,
They plot their dance while I just think.
A rubber plant wears shades so neat,
Struts down the aisle with tiny feet.

The herbs gossip of moonlit nights,
While radishes flex their leafy tights.
Persuading peas to join the game,
All under this bright electric flame.

They giggle softly, roots in sync,
Sharing secrets over a drink.
Life is grand in this cozy pot,
Who knew they'd love their sunny spot?

The Soft Touch of Artificial Ray

In the corner, a red bulb glows,
The lettuce struts, and off it goes.
Swaying gently, it takes the lead,
In this plastic jungle, they all heed.

The tomatoes sing a pop tune high,
Trying to reach the blazing sky.
While little sprouts with grand ambition,
Plot for fame with no submission.

A wandering vine starts a rap,
About its journey, oh what a map!
Drifting lazy, it makes a bed,
Now daily naps, who needs a spread?

Banana peels share the spotlight too,
Laughing at how their roles accrue.
Life's a stage under this technology,
All the plants with joyous ecology.

Petals Painted in Radiant Hues

Colorful blooms in a wacky spree,
Splashes of pink and bright jubilee.
A daisy giggles, 'Where's my friend?'
The garden's chaos seems to blend.

Sunflowers stand tall, making a scene,
Dressed in yellows, they all preen.
Naïve little weeds dance with flair,
Who knew photosynthesis could be so rare?

In every petal, a story told,
Of sunlight chased and secrets bold.
A marigold grins while on a fence,
Daring wallpaper to take a chance.

With every shade, another laugh spins,
As vibrant aisles draw silly grins.
Nature's palette, an artist's delight,
Making joy bloom in soft daylight.

The Elixir of Photons

Glowing bottles full of flair,
With liquid sun, what a hilarious affair.
Plants raise glasses, ready to toast,
'To the light show we all love most!'

Herbaceous friends with sassy roles,
Declare their love for those photon trolls.
While peppered leaves crack jokes galore,
Swapping puns while they ask for more.

Lettuce dreams of parmesan cheese,
Snickering at promises made with ease.
A zucchini prances, a humble star,
Jokes about being mistaken for a car.

With each bright flash, new tales arise,
Our leafy friends wearing veggie ties.
Who knew that elements could be so spry?
In this garden dance, we reach for the sky!

The Radiant Embrace

In a room with a rainbow glow,
Plants dance in lines, a circus show.
One leaf says, "I'm feeling bright!"
Another replies, "It's party night!"

With a stretch and a wiggle, they thrive,
Doing the cha-cha, feeling alive.
Roots are tapping to the beat,
Who knew soil could be so sweet?

Some leave say, "We're quite the crew!"
"Watch us grow, we'll outshine you!"
A little light, a splash of fun,
Watch us bloom; the race is on!

With pots stacked high like towers bold,
They whisper secrets, laughter untold.
Under the glow, they sway and cheer,
Growing together, year after year!

Lush Beneath the Luminance

A fuchsia flower in a fancy vase,
Chit-chats with a cactus, full of grace.
"Why so prickly?" the petals tease,
"It's my charm, it puts folks at ease!"

A broccoli dreams of being a tree,
While radishes giggle, "Just let it be!"
Lettuce shimmies, feeling fresh and spry,
While spinach whispers, "I'm quite the shy!"

Lights flicker; the party ignites,
Tiny sprouts join in with delights.
"Growing up is such a blast!"
"Let's hope our time isn't too fast!"

In this garden where laughter flows,
Every bloom has its tale that glows.
Together we thrive, we laugh, we play,
Under the brilliance, let's seize the day!

Growth in a Digital Dawn

In a world of pixels, plants take flight,
Green screens glimmer, oh what a sight!
"We're trending now, it's all the rage!"
"Tweeting our joy from the garden stage!"

A fern shares memes, the orchids laugh,
Remembering days of the old photograph.
"I once was frail, now I'm the star!"
"I've grown so much, just look at me, ha-ha!"

Hydroponics buzz like a busy hive,
Every leaf feels so gloriously alive.
Watch us upload our growth, so keen,
In a virtual world, we reign supreme!

Pixels and petals, a flashy display,
"Let's go viral!" the herbs shout, hooray!
Scrolling through blossoms, oh what a sight,
Flourishing blooms in the digital light!

Flora's Silhouette in Illumination

Shadows dance on the walls so bright,
Ferns and bulbs put on a light fight.
"Who's the fairest in this room?"
"I am, I am!" chants the blooming boom!

Sunflowers stretch, striking a pose,
While mint complains, "I can't even grow!"
"Just a little light, and I will shine!"
"Especially when I sip on sunshine!"

In this glow, we tell funny tales,
About the squirrel who raided our pales.
"Your roots are showing, oh what a sight!"
"At least I'm green, and that feels right!"

Each leaf grins, a tangled troupe,
Beneath the brilliance, they twist and swoop.
In this vivid world, together we thrive,
Dancing shadows come alive, we jive!

Vignettes of Verdant Life

In a realm where veggies dream,
The carrots plot their grand regime.
Tomatoes gossip in a row,
While radishes blush; what a show!

Peppers dance in merry heat,
They wiggle with a spicy beat.
Lettuce laughs, all crisp and cool,
As beans engage in playful duel.

With every leaf, a story spins,
In gardens where the chaos grins.
A tale of life, both strange and bright,
Where greens are kings and meals delight.

The sunbeam's giggle warms the soil,
As roots rejoice, they share their toil.
A veggie fête, with much ado,
In this patchwork life, all is askew!

Nature's Hidden Luminance

In corners where the shadows play,
A spinach wiggles, having its way.
Cucumbers dream of being cool,
While eggplants lounge in leafy school.

The broccoli is quite the sage,
Holding court with cabbage, scene of the stage.
Herbs throw confetti, fragrant and green,
As garlic giggles, unseen, unseen!

When garlic's fumes start taking flight,
The squirrels shout with pure delight.
They zip through rows, a fuzzy blur,
While peas attempt a pogo spur.

The sunlight spills sweet joy all 'round,
As veggies turn and gather sound.
In this salad's dance, they twirl and spin,
Life's a buffet, let's dig in!

The Tapestry of Growth

A tapestry of greens unfolds,
With stories only veggies hold.
The beets wear coats of scarlet cheer,
While zucchini flexes, growing near.

Datterino tomatoes throw a bash,
While cucumbers sneak in for a splash.
Corn talks tall, it's got the height,
Whispering secrets through the night.

The lettuce on the edge, so coy,
Dreams of being the gardener's joy.
As peas practice their acrobatic leaps,
While dreaming of farming's cozy heaps.

From tendrils to blossoms, life's a jest,
In this garden party, who needs to rest?
Nature's humor, in every sprout,
A world alive with joys about!

Glistening Edges of Leaves

Leaves glisten like they know a trick,
Each droplet dances, glittering quick.
Mint decides it's time to shine,
While thyme cracks jokes with the design.

A sunflower grins, all tall and bright,
Trying hard to catch the light.
Petunias giggle, throwing shade,
Oh, what a leafy escapade!

The peas are having quite the ball,
Hopping high, trying not to fall.
While carrots peer from earthy beds,
And plan their next big garden spreads.

The joyful hum of life is near,
As nature whispers soft and clear.
In this mirthful meadowland,
Every leaf with laughter stands!

The Glow of Possibility

In a room filled with flair, plants like to stare,
Green dreams reaching high, like they just don't care.
Leaves sway with a jig, under the buzzing beam,
Chatting with the bugs, living the plant dream.

Fertilizer tea parties, they sip with a grin,
Whispers of photosynthesis, let the fun begin!
Roots having a rave, twisting and turning,
While sunlight's their DJ, the energy's burning.

Lettuce wears a crown, feeling quite grand,
Basil talks in rhymes, isn't that just planned?
Chlorophyll the DJ, spinning tunes of green,
Every petal and leaf, a part of the scene.

In this leafy ballet, they twirl and they spin,
Complaining of soil stains, oh where to begin?
Nature's own circus, with a dash of delight,
Growing tall in the glow, they party all night.

Illuminated Urges

A pepper's doing yoga, stretching out its leaves,
While tomatoes gossip softly, flicking their sleeves.
Beans are on the move, they're dancing quite spry,
Swaying to the rhythm, oh me, oh my!

Cucumbers chuckle, they think they're so cool,
Claiming the title, 'Best Green Vegetable.'
Herbs are the cheerleaders, with pompoms in hand,
Chanting for growth, oh isn't it grand?

In this bright little world, where the light gets to play,
Mint wears a mustache, claiming 'Today's my day!'
Fungi are lurking, with their sneaky little schemes,
Hatching wild plans, living all of their dreams.

Even the dirt seems to laugh at their chase,
Each sprout with ambition, a smile on its face.
In this topsy-turvy, vibrant little lot,
The greens throw a party, giving it all they've got!

In the Warm Cloister

A cozy little scene, with greens all around,
Laughing with the shadows, in their sunlight found.
Ferns make a fort, with their feathery fronds,
While little seedlings break out, connecting beyond.

Cacti tell tall tales, of desert life so wild,
Sharing tales of rainstorms, oh how they smiled!
Moss gently chimes in, with a squishy old song,
In this warm little nook, where all plants belong.

Alright, they proclaim, let's have a grand feast,\nCabbage
brings the crunch, but green beans bring the least.
Peppers with their spice, add some flair to the fun,
While sage's wise words make all the chaos run.

As the glow fills the room, every bud aligns,
A party of growth, oh how brightly it shines!
In a world of green laughter, under warmth they thrive,
Together in their sanctuary, oh how they come alive!

Guardians of the Emerald Seed

In the garden retreat, seeds gather with glee,
Who'll sprout first in line, oh who can it be?
Each one tells a story, of growth yet untold,
In their emerald armor, brave and bold.

The radish plots mischief, with a wink in its eye,
While the timid spinach says, 'Oh me, oh my!'
Pumpkins roll about, telling tales of their size,
While carrots sneak snacks, in their sneaky disguise.

Together they giggle, their roots intertwined,
Against all the odds, in this world they find.
Sunshine is their ally, their steadfast guide,
Beneath this warm glow, they all take pride.

As night gently falls, they settle in peace,
Dreaming of vast gardens where troubles all cease.
Emerald warriors, with so much in store,
In this whimsical haven, they're ready for more!

Pathways of Radiant Roots

In the lab, it's quite a sight,
Plants wiggle with delight.
They've got a funny little dance,
Under beams, they prance and prance.

They speak in leafy whispers now,
As seedlings take a solemn vow.
To reach the top, they stretch and twist,
Making sure they won't be missed.

The earthworms watch, jaws wide in awe,
As zucchini shows off its leafy law.
In this green disco, they take a chance,
Hoping for a veggie romance.

But when the lights turn off at night,
They laugh and giggle out of sight.
With dreams of harvests, they take flight,
Under stars, their roots unite.

In the Halo of Germination

Sprouts emerge like starry knights,
Decked in green, they flex their tights.
In the halo, they pose in mirth,
Chasing the sun, for all it's worth.

Mighty peas in tiny shells,
Tell tales of leafy swells.
They giggle at their tiny friends,
While chasing dreams that never end.

Radishes play hopscotch in place,
While carrots juggle, just for grace.
A chorus of greens in silly jest,
Racing to see who's the best.

As darkness falls, they hold a ball,
In leafy gowns, they have a ball.
With roots entwined, they laugh and sway,
Dreaming of their bright, green day.

Glow of the Verdant Sanctuary

In a haven full of glee,
Tiny sprouts count one, two, three.
Glowing bright with silly flair,
They whisper "We don't have a care!"

Chives giggle in whispers sweet,
While lettuce prepares its leafy feat.
A dance party in the soil,
Where friends gather, steadfast and loyal.

Tomatoes wear a silly hat,
While peppers chat with a friendly spat.
In this sanctuary of green and fun,
The race to harvest has begun.

But when the lights flicker and go,
The plants assemble for a show.
Under the stars, they twirl about,
In nature's theater, they laugh out loud.

Blooming in the Spectrum

In a rainbow of colors bright,
Flowers bloom, pure delight.
Each petal wears a quirky smile,
As they flaunt their vibrant style.

Beyond the soil, a playful spark,
With marigolds that dance in the dark.
A tulip teases its tall friend,
Saying, "Watch this!" with a leafy bend.

Daisies throw a picnic bash,
While sunflowers play tag and dash.
In this spectrum of wild fun,
Each bloom prances under the sun.

Yet when sunset comes to call,
They sway together, one and all.
Telling stories of their day,
In dreams of bloom, they drift away.

Radiance of Green Hues

In a room full of plants, they're having a ball,
Basking in glory, they're standing tall.
With laughter and chatter, they whisper and sway,
Who knew that green could be so cliché?

The ferns tell jokes, their puns got me growing,
While succulents giggle, their laughter's quite glowing.
The monstera dances, with a leaf like a sail,
Claiming the title of funniest tale.

Cacti roll their eyes, so prickly and sly,
While others tease them, oh my, oh my!
A jungle soirée, where each one is keen,
Who knew being green could be such a scene?

In light that is bright, their colors unwind,
A riot of shades, a comical find.
With each little stem, they play their own tune,
In this leafy cabaret, we'll dance till the moon.

Veins of Light and Leaf

Two leafy friends share a sunbeam's embrace,
With veins like highways, they race through the space.
"I'm chlorophyll-rich, what about you?"
"A little more light, and I'd make a brew!"

The leaves start to giggle, their humor is grand,
"You think you're so hot, but I'm cooler, you'll stand!"
A dance of green fibers, their laughter ignites,
As sunlight comes pouring, they claim their rights.

A stem bends and teases, "Hey, check out my flair!"
But tipsy from photons, it tumbles in air.
"My party's in full swing, don't let it go!
Join the fun of the frames in this radiant show!"

With each playful poke, they gather the cheer,
Under beams of bright laughter, all life seems so clear.
Veins of light carry tales of joy and glee,
In the garden of giggles, we're all wild and free.

Fables of Flora and Illumination

In the garden of whispers, a tale gets unfurled,
Where petunias gossip and daisies are twirled.
"Have you heard the latest on the Marigold streak?"
"Oh please! They think they're hotter, they're just so unique!"

The herbs start a rumor, it's spicy and true,
While the roses roll over, they've caught a smell too.
"Oh darling, your petals are simply divine!"
Yet, wilted in laughter, they chuckle in line.

A tall sunflower shouts, "I'm tallest, it's clear!"
But the tiny bluebells claim, "We're the ones near!"
In fables of flora, with comical sights,
They emit pure joy in the glow of their lights.

So join in the fun, where the plants sway and play,
In this vibrant domain, who needs words anyway?
With laughter as soil, and friendship the seed,
In the tales of green life, we all intercede.

A Symphony in the Smallest Leaves

In a tiny green corner, a concert unfolds,
With the smallest of leaves, bold stories are told.
A violin leaf hums, conducting the night,
While the others all chime in, oh what a sight!

The tiniest sprout offers a shy little solo,
But soon finds its rhythm, a true green kiddo.
"Don't fret about size, just feel the delight!"
As they twirl in unison, a magical flight.

With a flourish of ferns, a crescendo appears,
While the moss joins the beat, tapping roots with cheer.
The air fills with laughter, a symphonic spree,
As the green, leafy creatures weave joy over glee.

So raise up your pots to this leafy ballet,
Each plant plays a part in its own wacky way.
With chlorophyll chords and sunlight on lanes,
In the greenest of spaces, fun flourishes, remains.

Where Light and Leaf Coalesce

In a room of green and fluorescent buzz,
Plants gather round just because.
They dance and sway, quite the sight,
Under the glow, they're feeling light.

Ferns don hats made of paper plates,
While succulents flirt with their mates.
A cactus grins, all spiky and sly,
"Take a picture, I'm ready to fly!"

The beans are chatting, full of jest,
"I can sprout faster than all the rest!"
Batch after batch in comical cheer,
"Let's throw a party, everyone's here!"

And as the bulbs flicker high and bright,
The herbs all roll in their leafy delight.
Under this silly, gleeful expanse,
Who knew growing could be such a dance!

Verse of the Vibrant Canopy

A leafy brigade, united in glow,
Little green soldiers, in a neat row.
The basil whispers, "I smell so fine!"
"I was made for pasta, I'm ready to dine!"

In the corner, a rogue pot acts bold,
Claims to be 'the best'—if truth be told.
"I've got the scent of fresh lemonade,"
While the others chuckle at the fruit parade.

A bean stalk's reaching for the ceiling fan,
"Just one more inch, I'm the tallest man!"
With each leaf stretching, big dreams arise,
In this vibrant space, they're quite the prize.

So here's to the grow lights and quirky cheer,
Where the greens unite and have no fear.
For each vibrant leaf under shimmer and sway,
Lives a tale that's funny, day after day.

The Aromatic Touch of Light

Oregano winks with a twist of lime,
"Who needs sunshine when we've got rhyme?"
The thyme adds sass, "Let's spice up the night!"
In this leafy party, they twinkle and bright.

Pots of mint insist they're quite refined,
"Brew us in tea, we're one of a kind!"
With each little whisper, they share their plight,
"Beneath these tubes, life feels just right!"

Pansies pout, "Why don't we sing?"
"Maybe then someone will bring us a fling!"
"Only if we promise to keep it cool,
No bickering here, we've got the school!"

Laughter erupts from the chlorophyll crowd,
Creativity blooms; they're feeling quite proud.
With the scent of the garden wafting around,
In this whimsical realm, pure joy is found.

The Solstice of Sprouts

Gather 'round for a sprouty affair,
Under gleaming bulbs, without a care.
Lettuce leaps with jubilant flair,
It's a solstice of greens, a fragrant fair!

Radishes boast, "We're roots of renown!"
While peppers blush in their colorful gown.
Chickadees chirp just outside the door,
"Invite us in; we'll dance on the floor!"

The chillies chuckle, "Spicy today!"
Snickering leafies, they banter and play.
Each sprout contributes to the scrumptious stew,
In this indoor garden, humor's the glue.

As the lights dim low, the fun's not done,
They toast to the bulbs and their vibrant run.
Under the shimmer of light's sweet embrace,
It's a sprout celebration—what a glorious place!

In the Shelter of Radiance

In the glow of my funky lamp,
Plants jive like they're at a camp.
They sway and twist in dazzling light,
Who knew a leaf could dance all night?

Cacti in sequins, so bold and bright,
Proudly show off their spiky might.
Even the herbs are in the groove,
Waving their leaves, making me move!

Growth Under Illuminated Skies

Under the glow, things start to sprout,
Potatoes practicing the dance about.
Tomatoes gossiping with a smile,
"Let's take selfies, wait a while!"

The basil's busting out some flair,
Telling the others, "I just don't care!"
Ferns tease the beans, "Aren't we fab?"
Leafy greens just hum, "Oh, grab a cab!"

Shadows of Verdant Dreams

In shadows long, there's giggling grass,
Yielding puns like an aging sass.
"Lettuce leaf together, we'll thrive,"
In this bright world, we're so alive!

Oh, the seedlings plot a daring heist,
"Steal the spotlight, let's twist it nice!"
With roots entwined in a playful brawl,
They laugh so loud, they've grown so tall!

Cultivated Cradles

In pots where whispers hilariously bloom,
Little sprouts chat, "We'll take the room!"
With every sunbeam, they stretch and yawn,
"Let's write a book—'How to be a Lawn!'"

Carrots are teasing, "I'm digging in deep!"
While herbs argue over who's got the leap.
In this garden, laughter grows so wide,
With a sprinkle of humor, our plants take pride!

Greenery in the Glow

In the kitchen corner, plants all aligned,
They chat and gossip, oh, the stories unwind.
Ferns trade secrets with the herbs so spry,
While cacti giggle as they watch the time fly.

Each leaf a comedian, with a punchline to share,
The basil's a joker, the mint pulls a dare.
In their radiant haven, under luminescent skies,
They plot silly pranks, what a riot, oh my!

Even succulents smirk, puffed up with pride,
With their thick little tummies, they can't help but ride.
On waves of warm light, they sway and they tease,
"Hey, come on, humans, let's have some fun, please!"

A raucous affair, this glow-lit retreat,
Where the greenery dances to a rhythmic beat.
They may just be plants, but they sure can delight,
In this cozy corner, all chaos feels right.

The Sublime Pulse of Growth

A tomato winks as it swells with delight,
It flexes its skin, soaking up all that light.
Carrots are dancing, though buried in dirt,
"Just wait till you see us, we're ready to flirt!"

Radishes chuckle, poking out their heads,
"Life's like a veggie, it's all in the spreads!"
With roots intertwined, they form a tight crew,
Who knew farming could be so much fun, who knew?

In this small jungle, the laughter flows free,
"Is that a weed?" asks the thyme, "Oh dear me!"
The herbs throw a party, all flavors collide,
Their best punch is served with a sprig of pride.

So here's to the growth, let hilarity reign,
In this bustling patch, joy is never mundane.
With each little sprout, a new story unfolds,
In this whimsical world, laughter never grows old.

Harvesting the Light

The sunbeams argue over who's taking charge,
While veggies bathe in radiance, oh how they enlarge!
With cucumbers plotting their next big escape,
They laugh, "Tonight's salad will have a new shape!"

The peppers are preening, colors shining so bright,
"C'mon, make us salsa, we're ready to bite!"
But onions just laugh, with their layers so bold,
"Chop us up gently, we're treasures to hold!"

Fruits hanging heavy, in a carnival show,
"Catch me if you can!" shouts a cheeky mango.
While pumpkins conspire to start a parade,
Their orange army forms, it's a ghostly charade!

So come join the harvest in this raucous abode,
Where laughter is served with a side of good code.
For under this brightness, we'll dance and we'll play,
In the bounty of light, we'll brighten the day.

The Secret Lives of Leaves

Leaves whisper secrets that flutter and float,
"Did you hear the one about the cabbage?" they gloat.
With every little rustle, they share juicy tales,
In this leafy society, everybody prevails.

"Lettuce suggests, 'Let's turn on the charm!'
While spinach just laughs, unruffled and calm.
A bouncy old fern struts in with flair,
"Keep up with me, friends! I've got so much hair!"

The ivy plans pranks, climbing up on the wall,
"Let's wrap around humans, and watch them all fall!"
While sage reminisces, "Remember that time?
We were picked for the stew? Oh my, was it prime!"

In this lively green hub, where laughter is the key,
Leaves shine with humor, wild and carefree.
They know how to grow, and to giggle with ease,
In this secret life of leaves, there's joy in the breeze.

Melodies of Transcendent Green

In the corner, plants do sway,
Each leaf a dancer, bold display.
With roots that wiggle, grow, and twine,
They gossip secrets, all divine.

The cactus hums a little tune,
While ferns frolic under the moon.
Their chlorophyll, a vibrant cheer,
A botanical party, oh dear!

The spider plant tells a tall tale,
Of how it outgrew last summer's gale.
With vines like snakes, they twist and play,
Their laughter echoes day by day.

Oh, leafy comrades, bright and spry,
With every breeze, you wave hi-fi.
In this jungle of pots and glee,
We're all just plants, wild and free!

A Dance in the Night's Light

Under a glow that's far from subtle,
My sunflowers perform a huddle.
With petals bright, they shimmy right,
And twirl like dancers, oh what a sight!

The basil's got moves, you have to see,
With pirouettes as fresh as can be.
Tomatoes tumble, ripe and round,
Creating chaos, frolic abound.

The lettuce laughs with crispy flair,
As radishes roll like they just don't care.
In this leafy cabaret, what a show!
Who knew veggies could steal the glow?

So join the fun, let's all sway,
In a garden where plants run the ballet.
With roots in tune and blooms that jive,
We're all alive, oh, how we thrive!

Cultivating Illuminated Dreams

In pots of joy where laughter grows,
The carrots dream in tidy rows.
They whisper softly, 'We're the best,'
While peas contest, 'We trump the rest!'

At night they wiggle, roots in bed,
With radish stories in their head.
"Oh, what a day!" the herbs all sigh,
As moonbeams dance and fireflies fly.

The crew of greens hums songs so sweet,
While tiny sprouts tap their little feet.
With every droplet, cheers abound,
In this garden party underground!

Forget the sun, bring on the glow,
These dreams are lit, come one, come flow.
With laughter sprouting all around,
We'll cultivate joy in happy ground!

The Auras of Green Life

With stems aglow and leaves so bright,
The jungle feels just right tonight.
A margarita plant sips on cheer,
While peas share tales we long to hear.

The kale's a joker, spiking the fun,
With lettuce quips that weigh a ton.
The thyme just rolls, it hardly cares,
Its fragrant jokes float through the airs.

Cacti boast with their prickly charm,
While sunflowers beam, they mean no harm.
A riot of greens, a laugh parade,
In garden antics, we're all displayed.

So here we are, a vibrant crew,
With secret gigs and pranks anew.
In every leaf, a story hides,
In this green realm, where laughter bides!

Sowing Seeds of Illumination

In a pot, I place a seed,
Hoping for a leafy deed.
A sprinkle here, a little cheer,
Will I grow veggies or a curious deer?

I talk to my plants, they seem to smirk,
"Water us right, or we'll go berserk!"
First a sprout, then a big surprise,
Tomatoes do challenge my cooking ties.

They stretch and dance, a leafy parade,
Confused, I wonder, did I overtrade?
With sunlight bright, oh what a sight,
I swear my garden holds a nightly light!

So here I stand with shovel in hand,
Digging for treasure in my backyard land.
Will they bloom into laughter or a full-on riot?
Stay tuned, my friends, for the veggie diet!

Dance of the Urban Botanical

In the city where concrete reigns,
Grow lights sparkle, ignoring the chains.
Potted herbs wear shades of green,
As they groove to a rhythm unseen.

Cacti wobble, succulents sway,
In this dance-off, they steal the day.
"I'm a cactus, it's not a facade,
But watch me twist—I'm a prickly charade!"

The basil hums a tune so sweet,
With parsley and mint, they're quite the feat.
They gather close for a foliage ball,
Who knew greens could have a gall?

At night they sing, the air is bright,
Plants in a concert, oh what a sight!
Chlorophyll dreams in the urban glow,
If only the neighbors could see this show!

Illuminated Growth

In a room where shadows play,
Little sprouts find their way.
They stretch and yawn, oh what a scene,
Wondering if they can be seen.

Under bulbs that shine like suns,
Dancing plants, oh what fun runs!
"Am I a lettuce or a radish?" they muse,
"Betting on you, I've got nothing to lose!"

The peas wear hats, the carrots are bold,
Each leaf telling stories untold.
"Oh, let's party, it's all we crave,
Grab the light, do the plant rave!"

They twirl and spin, each in their pot,
Claiming the space, giving it a shot.
In this little green world so bright,
A riot of joy takes flight each night!

Echoes of Nature's Glow

A little light whispers secrets near,
As my garden tries to commandeer.
"Hello, little sapling, how's the view?
Planning world domination, are you?"

In this lively patch, laughter spreads,
As daisies tell jokes, spinning their heads.
The radish grins, "I'm not just a treat,
Best root in town, can't be beat!"

A leafy affair, under the bright beam,
In a world of greens, they're living the dream.
"Let's grow big, let's be chummy!
With our leafy friends, we'll make it all funny!"

So gather round, hear nature's song,
Under electric stars, it won't be long.
From tiny seeds to laughter's glow,
In this pot, who knows how far we'll grow!

www.ingramcontent.com/pod-product-compliance
Lightning Source LLC
Chambersburg PA
CBHW070321120526
44590CB00017B/2771